GET SMART ABOUT

DR. SEUSS

Rocket Books

Get Smart about Dr. Seuss
by Adam Kent

Published by Rocket Books, Inc.
New York, NY, USA

For kids...
who dream big,
who work hard to become better,
who get up when they fall,
who know we are all human and
all worthy of respect and success.

For my son Little Adam...
who lights up my life.

May your dreams come true.

This book is for you.

ABOUT THIS BOOK

This biography book is meant to be a fun, brief and inspirational look at the life of a famous person. Reading biographies can help learn from people who have experienced extraordinary things. While you read through the books in this series, think about how their experiences can help you in your own life!

As you read this book you will find bolded words. There are definitions of the words at the end of each page. You will also find interesting facts at the end of each chapter. Plus, there are some questions to get you thinking at the end of the book.

I hope you enjoy learning about this extraordinary person!

Have a great time reading,

Adam Kent

CONTENTS

ADAM KENT

GET SMART ABOUT
DR. SEUSS

Rocket Books

DR. SEUSS
AT A GLANCE

Dr. Seuss was a famous author and illustrator who wrote and drew many fun and exciting children's books. He wrote over 60 books in his lifetime, including popular titles like "The Cat in the Hat," "Green Eggs and Ham," and "Oh, the Places You'll Go!" Kids and grown-ups alike love his stories because they are filled with silly characters, rhyming words, and bright and colorful illustrations. Dr. Seuss will always be remembered as one of the most beloved and successful children's book authors of all time.

DR. SEUSS
FAST FACTS

1. Dr. Seuss was a pen name for Theodor Geisel, who was a famous author and illustrator.

2. His books are known for their rhyming and silly characters, like the Cat in the Hat and the Grinch.

3. Some of his most famous books include "Green Eggs and Ham," "The Cat in the Hat," and "Oh, The Places You'll Go!"

4. Dr. Seuss never had any children, despite being such a children's book author.

5. Dr. Seuss was born on March 2nd, and his birthday is celebrated every year as Read Across America Day. Kids all over the country read his books on this special day!

CHAPTER 1

THE EARLY DAYS

Dr. Seuss, whose real name was Theodor Geisel, was born in Springfield, Massachusetts in 1904. His parents were Theodor Robert Geisel and Henrietta Seuss Geisel.

Theodor Robert Geisel was of German descent. He was a successful brewer and later became the superintendent of parks and forestry in Springfield.

Henrietta Seuss Geisel was of German ancestry as well. She stayed at home to raise Theodore and her children. He had two older sisters, Marnie and Henrietta.

Despite the family's wealth, they lived a simple life. They were a religious family. They were Lutheran Christians. In fact, Dr. Seuss remained a Lutheran throughout his life.

Growing up, Dr. Seuss lived in a large Victorian home that had a big backyard with plenty of space to play. Both of his parents were supportive of their children's interests and education. They also had a love for music, books, and the arts, which they passed down to their children.

His parents encouraged his creativity and love of learning from a young age. They frequently took the children on trips to the library. They exposed them to different cultures through travel to places like Germany, France, and Switzerland. This helped inspire Dr. Seuss's love for different cultures and languages.

As a child, Dr. Seuss was active and adventurous. He enjoyed spending time outside, exploring nearby woods, and playing with his friends. He was also a big fan of the circus. He would often go to see performances with his family.

Dr. Seuss was also imaginative. He enjoyed playing with his toy trains, and he would build elaborate structures with blocks. Most of all, he loved reading books. He was especially drawn to the fantastical stories of writers like Lewis Carroll, who wrote "Alice's Adventures in Wonderland," and Jules Verne, who wrote "Journey to the Center of the Earth."

Dr. Seuss always had a close relationship with his sister Marnie throughout his life. He often said that she helped inspire his love of writing and storytelling. Sadly, His sister Henrietta died at a very young age, when he was only four years old.

Marnie was a talented artist. She often encouraged him to pursue his creative interests. One of his creative interests was music.

Dr. Seuss played the piano and even composed his own pieces.

Dr. Seuss went to public school in Springfield where he was born. He showed an early talent for drawing and writing. He was an excellent student. He was also a talented athlete. He played a variety of different sports.

During his teenage years, Dr. Seuss attended Dartmouth College. There, he developed his love for writing and drawing. At school was known for his quick **wit** and humor. He quickly made a name for himself on campus as a talented cartoonist. He often used his cartoons to make fun of his

---

wit /wɪt/ noun: the ability to use words and ideas in a clever and amusing way <example: He is known for his quick wit and humor.>

teachers and classmates! Despite this mischievous streak, Dr. Seuss was a good student and well-liked by his peers.

At college, Dr. Seuss took art classes and joined the school's yearbook staff. He also worked for the Dartmouth Jack-O-Lantern humor magazine. as editor-in-chief and in charge of comics.

One little-known fact is that it was during his time at Dartmouth that he first came up with the name "Dr. Seuss" and started using it. The story is interesting... Dr. Seuss was actually caught drinking alcohol. He wasn't supposed to be! This was during a time called the "Prohibition." when alcohol was

forbidden by law. The Prohibition lasted from 1920-1933.

As punishment for drinking, Dr. Seuss was ordered to stop all of his **extracurricular** activities. Dr. Seuss really wanted to continue his activities and keep drawing comics, so he came up with an idea to solve the problem. He started using the name, "Seuss" as a **pseudonym**, so no one would know

---

extracurricular /ˌek-strə-kə-ˈri-kyə-lər/ adjective: outside the normal curriculum or routine <example: She participates in several extracurricular activities, including sports and music.>

forbidden /fər-ˈbɪ-dən/ adjective: not allowed by law, rule, or custom <example: Smoking is forbidden in this building.>

pseudonym /ˈsoō-də-nəm/ noun: a name used by a writer or artist instead of their real name <example: He writes under a pseudonym to protect his privacy.>

he was still working there! It worked! Can you believe it?

After Dartmouth, he also attended a college called Lincoln College for his graduate studies. Graduate studies are studies after college. His university was in Oxford, England. He initially attended the school with the intention of pursuing a doctoral degree in literature. However, his plan took an unexpected turn when he met Helen Palmer, who would later become his first wife.

Helen encouraged Dr. Seuss to explore a career in art rather than continuing, redirecting his focus toward illustration and storytelling. Although he did not earn a formal advanced degree, his time in

Oxford had a big impact on his artistic development.

CHAPTER 1
FUN FACTS

1. Dr. Seuss loved to draw and make up stories even as a young boy.

2. His real name was Theodor Geisel, but he later adopted the pen name "Dr. Seuss."

3. Dr. Seuss loved to travel and would often go on trips with his family, which inspired his love for different cultures and languages.

4. He loved to read and was inspired by the works of his favorite authors.

5. He went to Dartmouth College, where he became the editor-in-chief of the college humor magazine.

CHAPTER 2
FAMILY MATTERS

Theodor Robert Geisel, better known as Dr. Seuss's father, was born in 1879. He was the son of German American parents. He grew up in Springfield, Massachusetts, where he married Henrietta Seuss in 1901.

Theodor was tall and athletic, with black hair and a moustache. He was a skilled **marksman**. In fact, in 1902, he held the world title for target shooting at 200 yards.

Theodor was the President of Springfield Breweries, his father's business. In 1920, the sale of alcohol became illegal, so he could no longer keep the brewery open. After, he became the Superintendent of Parks for the city of Springfield, which included running the Forest Park Zoo.

Dr. Seuss often visited Forest Park with his family. There they would walk the trails, fish, and visit the zoo. These visits helped to spark his love of nature and

---

marksman /'märk-mən/ noun: a person who is skilled in shooting, especially with a rifle <example: He is a marksman who competes in shooting competitions.>

animals, which he would later **incorporate** into his books. Throughout his childhood, his father was a big influence on his creativity and imagination. He encouraged his son's artistic side from a young age.

Even though he had a lot of **professional pursuits**, Dr. Seuss's

---

incorporate /ɪn-ˈkɔr-pə-rāt/ verb: to combine or join different elements or parts to form a single entity <example: The company incorporated new technology into its products.>

professional /prə-ˈfə-shə-nəl/ adjective: relating to or belonging to a profession <example: She is a professional dancer who performs in ballets.>

pursuits /pər-ˈsü-ts/ noun: an activity or interest that one enjoys and follows <example: Her hobbies include outdoor pursuits such as hiking and camping.>

dad was a family man who loved to spend time with his wife and children. He was a kind and caring man who always encouraged his children to follow their dreams and pursue their passions. Despite the difficulties he faced in his own life, he remained optimistic and focused on the positive aspects of life, which his son would later reflect in his books.

Dr. Seuss's mother, Henrietta Seuss, was the daughter of Bavarian immigrants. Bavaria is an area in what is now Germany. Growing up, Henrietta was forced to give up her dreams of attending college. Instead, she had to work in her family's bakery. She made sure that her children had the opportunity to go to college.

Henrietta was a musical woman. She sang to her children at night. She also helped to develop their love of rhythm, rhyme, and words.

Dr. Seuss had two sisters. One was Henrietta, and the other was Marnie. One of the sad memories of Dr. Seuss's childhood was the loss of his youngest sister, Henrietta. She was born in 1906 and named after their mother but died of pneumonia at the young age of 18 months. The memory of his sister's death stayed with Dr. Seuss throughout his life, and he later wrote about it in a biography.

Dr. Seuss had a close relationship with his older sister, Margaretha Christine, who was affectionately known as Marnie.

Marnie was the firstborn of the three siblings and had a significant impact on Dr. Seuss's childhood. She was very studious, took her schoolwork seriously, and later graduated magna cum laude from her high school. This means she graduated "with great praise." After high school, she went to a college called Smith College.

In contrast to his sister Marnie, Dr. Seuss was more creative and imaginative, spending much of his time drawing and making up stories. Despite their differences, Marnie and Dr. Seuss had a close relationship. They would often play together, go to the zoo, and attend birthday parties together.

Overall, Dr. Seuss's childhood was filled with love, support, and creativity. He was surrounded by a close-knit family who encouraged his imagination and creativity. His experiences in Forest Park and the Forest Park Zoo helped to shape his unique and imaginative writing style. The loss of his youngest sister was a tragedy that stayed with him throughout his life, but overall, his childhood was filled with happy memories of playing with his sister, Marnie, and his close relationship with his parents. These experiences helped to shape the talented and imaginative author and **illustrator** Dr. Seuss became.

---

illustrator /ɪ-ˈlʌs-trə-tər/ noun: a person who creates illustrations, especially for books or magazines <example: The book was illustrated by a famous illustrator.>

CHAPTER 2
FUN FACTS

1. Dr. Seuss had two sisters, Margaretha and Henrietta.

2. His family was of German American descent.

3. Dr. Seuss's father was a successful businessman who ran a brewery and later became the Superintendent of Parks in Springfield, Massachusetts.

4. Dr. Seuss's mother was a homemaker and sang her

children to sleep with rhyming songs.

5. Dr. Seuss loved to draw and was inspired by the animals he saw at the Forest Park Zoo near his home.

CHAPTER 3
A UNIQUE EDUCATION

Dr. Seuss's educational journey began in Springfield Public Schools. He attended Central High School. He was a good student in high school. However, he was especially creative and loved to draw and write.

After high school, Dr. Seuss went on to attend Dartmouth

College in Hanover, New Hampshire. While at Dartmouth, he continued to develop his artistic talents by drawing cartoons for the school's **humor** magazine, Jack-O-Lantern. He also became a member of the Dartmouth College theater group and performed in several productions.

Dr. Seuss's college years were not without challenges. If you remember, he was caught drinking alcohol, which was against the rules. He was asked to leave the magazine. This was a major disappointment for him. He wanted to continue to draw cartoons for

---

humor /ˈhyü-mər/ noun: the quality of being amusing or comical <example: He has a great sense of humor and always makes people laugh.>

the magazine, so he came up with the idea of using a fake name. He wrote under the pseudonym "Seuss." This name was inspired by his mother's name, Henrietta Seuss.

After graduating from Dartmouth in 1925, Dr. Seuss went on to attend Oxford University in England as a scholarship student. He intended to earn a Ph.D., which is the highest degree you can earn. He studied English literature, but he left Oxford in 1927 before completing his degree. There is a rumor that he left due to a disagreement with his professor over his thesis. Despite this, his time at Oxford greatly influenced his writing and artistic style.

In addition to his formal education, Dr. Seuss was also a lifelong learner. He traveled widely and was always curious about the world around him. This sense of wonder and adventure can be seen in his books! Throughout his books, characters explore strange and fantastical places, meeting new and unusual creatures along the way. This is kind of like what he did in real life!

CHAPTER 3
FUN FACTS

1. Dr. Seuss attended Dartmouth College in Hanover, New Hampshire, where he was the editor-in-chief of the Jack-O-Lantern, the school's humor magazine.

2. Dr. Seuss went to graduate school at Lincoln College, Oxford in England. However, he did not complete his degree and left the college in 1927.

3. He studied English Literature while at Lincoln College and intended to get a PhD.

CHAPTER 4

A CAREER TO REMEMBER

In 1927, Dr. Seuss left Oxford, England without a degree and decided to start his career earlier than he had expected in the United States. He wanted to make it as a writer and illustrator, so he started submitting his work to various magazines, book publishers, and advertising agencies. He was rejected in the beginning. However, he got his first big break when he sold a cartoon to The Saturday Evening Post.

New York City

Soon after, he moved to New York City where he landed a job as a writer and illustrator for a humor magazine called Judge. It was about six months after starting at Judge that Dr. Seuss's published his first professional work. He published it under the pen name "Dr. Seuss." If you remember, he had first used "Seuss" in college.

However, this time, he added the "Dr."

At this time, Dr. Seuss was able to marry his girlfriend, Helen Palmer. His successes provided him with a **stable** income. He felt secure making that step.

Dr. Seuss continued to work at for Judge until one fateful day. One of Dr. Seuss's cartoons for Judge mentioned a company called Flit. Flit was a common bug spray at the time made by Standard Oil of New Jersey. Apparently, the wife of a boss at Flit saw his cartoon while getting her hair done. She liked it and urged her husband to sign him. Her

---

stable /'stā-bəl/ adjective: not likely to change or collapse; steady <example: The economy has been stable for several years.>

husband was also impressed and signed Dr. Seuss right away to create ads for Flit.

Dr. Seuss's ad was a hit. It ran for a long time from 1928 until 1941. It became so popular that people started recognizing Dr. Seuss and his work, and big companies started hiring him for their own ads. He was hired by big companies at the time like Life, Liberty, and Vanity Fair.

Dr. Seuss earned more from his advertising work than even his most successful Dartmouth classmates.

Dr. Suess rose up in the social ranks because of his success. He continued working for big companies in addition to continuing with Standard oil like Ford Motor Company, NBC Radio Network, and Holly Sugar.

In 1931, Dr. Seuss Wrote his first book called "Boners." Boners was a collection of children's sayings that he had illustrated. It was published by Viking Press in 1931. The book was a big success. It even made it to the top of The New York Times non-fiction bestseller list! Soon after, he published a second called "More Boners."

Because he was so successful with these first two books, Dr. Seuss wrote and illustrated an ABC book featuring "very strange animals." This time his book was not a big success. This didn't stop Dr. Seuss from continuing his writing!

In the early 1930s, Dr. Seuss and his wife traveled a lot. Within the first half of the **decade**, they had traveled to over 30 countries! Can you believe it? They had enough money, and Dr. Seuss also felt that traveling helped his creativity and his writing.

In 1936, Dr. Seuss and his wife were coming back from Europe on a boat. The sound of the engines inspired him to write a poem which then became his first ever kids' book, "And to Think That I Saw It on Mulberry Street." Unfortunately, when he tried to get it published,

---

decade /ˈdɛ-kād/ noun: a period of ten years <example: The last decade has seen significant changes in technology.>

between 20-43 publishers rejected it! He was about to give up when an old friend from college helped get it published by a company called Vanguard Press. After that, he wrote four more books before World War II started. These included "The 500 Hats of Bartholomew Cubbins," "The King's Stilts," "The Seven Lady Godivas," and "Horton Hatches the Egg."

World War II

When World War II started, Dr. Seuss started to focus on politics and the war, looking for ways to express his beliefs and take action. He started making political cartoons for a newspaper called

PM. He drew over 400 of them in just two years. He used his cartoons to criticize leaders like Hitler and Mussolini. He also made cartoons that showed how racism was hurting the war effort.

Later on in the war, he even joined the US army as a captain and worked on making posters and films to help. He wrote some films about peace after the war and made army training films. He was even awarded a special award called the Legion of Merit! One of the films he wrote became the basis for a movie that eventually won an Academy Award. Another film, called "Gerald McBoing-Boing," was based on one of his stories and also won an Academy Award.

Children's Books

After the war, Dr. Seuss and his wife moved to La Jolla, California. There, he started writing children's books again. He worked with two top publishing companies. In the following years, he wrote tons of books including some worldwide favorites like "If I Ran the Zoo" (1950), "Horton Hears a Who!" (1955), "The Cat in the Hat" (1957), "How the Grinch Stole Christmas!" (1957), and "Green Eggs and Ham" (1960). He also made a movie called "The 5,000 Fingers of Dr. T," which came out in 1953, but it didn't do well. In the 1950s, he wrote some short stories that were published in magazines, some of which got turned into books later on.

The Cat in the Hat

One interesting story about Dr. Seuss's writing experience is about how he wrote perhaps his most famous book, "The Cat in the Hat." Dr. Seuss was asked to write a book that would be easy for kids to read. A report had come out that said kids weren't learning to read because the books were too boring. So, a man named William Ellsworth Spaulding, who worked for a publishing company, gave Dr. Seuss a list of 348 words and asked him to write a book using 236 of those words only. "The Cat in the Hat" was the result of that assignment. The book was a big hit!

Awards

Throughout his career, he won lots of awards. In 1955, Dr. Seuss was awarded an honorary doctorate from Dartmouth College. He joked that he would now have to sign "Dr. Dr. Seuss." Later, he got another honorary degree from Whittier College in 1980. He even won a Pulitzer Prize in 1984 for his contributions to children's literature. This is one of the most **prestigious** awards that he could

---

prestigious /pre-ˈsti-jə-wəs/ adjective: respected and admired because of achievement, reputation, or social status <example: The university is one of the most prestigious in the country.>

have received.

Before Dr. Seuss died in 1991, he had written and illustrated over 60 children's books. Over 600 million copies of his books have been sold. Dr. Seuss became one of the most successful and **influential** children's book authors of all time. Today, his books continue to be read and enjoyed by children all over the world.

---

influential /ɪn-ˈflü-ən(t)-shəl/ adjective: having the power to influence or affect change <example: He is an influential person in the community, known for his leadership and ideas.>

CHAPTER 4
FUN FACTS

1. Dr. Seuss wrote and illustrated over 60 books for children.

2. His first children's book, "And to Think That I Saw It on Mulberry Street," was published in 1937.

3. Dr. Seuss's most famous book is "The Cat in the Hat," which was published in 1957.

4. Dr. Seuss's books have been translated into many different languages and have sold over 600 million copies worldwide.

5. He won many awards for his books, including the Pulitzer Prize.

HOBBIES AND PASSIONS

Dr. Seuss had a range of hobbies that contributed to his imaginative creations. Beyond his writing and illustrating, he had a deep love for art, playing a role in shaping his unique visual style.

Dr. Seuss was also an avid collector of hats, which inspired the hats worn by characters in his books. He had several hundred hats from around the world and started collecting them in the 1930s. One of his hats was a genuine viking helmet! Dr. Seuss also had a large collection of paintings. He kept his hats and paintings in a secret closet in his home.

Dr. Seuss's lesser-known hobby of taxidermy sheds light on his unique creative process. Taxidermy is the art of preserving dead animals by stuffing them into lifelike form. Dr. Seuss's father worked at the Springfield Zoo and then as superintendent of parks. When animals from the parks passed away, his father would send parts like horns, bills, and antlers to Dr. Seuss's New York apartment. There, using these remains from the animal kingdom, he crafted 17 extraordinary, sculpted creatures in the 1930s. These creations weren't like your typical taxidermy. They were invented creatures that showed off Dr. Seuss's creative spirit.

Before Dr. Seuss became a published children's book author, he was written about in a magazine because of these creations. In 1938, Look magazine wrote about him, calling him, "The World's Most Eminent Authority on Unheard-Of Animals." Not all reactions to his creations were positive. One reporter described visiting Dr. Seuss's creations as possibly causing nightmares for some people!

Dr. Seuss's hobbies weren't just for fun; they actively shaped his creative side. His hobbies not only provided him with enjoyment but also left a mark on the world, reminding us of all of the importance of embracing our passions to foster creativity and inspire others.

Beyond his hobbies, Dr. Seuss was also a champion of **charitable** causes throughout his life. He had reached wealth and success in his career, and he wanted to give back. In 1958, Dr. Seuss created the Dr. Seuss Foundation. Over the

---

charitable /ˈchar-ə-tə-bəl/ adjective: relating to giving money, help, or time to those in need <example: She is known for her charitable work in the community.>

years, the foundation has donated over $300 million to various organizations focused on education, environmental conservation, and health.

Education

The Dr. Seuss Foundation gave a lot to Dartmouth College, where Dr. Seuss went to college. There they helped **establish** the Geisel School of Medicine. The foundation has supported the University of California, San Diego, as well. They created the Geisel Library which

---

establish /ɪ-'stab-lɪʃ/ verb: to create or set up a system, organization, or institution <example: They established a new company to produce the product.>

holds nearly 10,000 Dr. Seuss items.

Environment

Dr. Seuss's love of animals and the environment also inspired his giving. The foundation has given a lot to the Scripps Institution of Oceanography, a leading institution in the study of climate change. They also helped establish several areas of the San Diego Zoo and Wild Animal Park, including the Elephant Odyssey and the Lion Wading Pool. One of the zoo's elephants was even named Ingadze, or Horton in English, after Dr. Seuss's character in "Horton Hears a Who!"

Health

Dr. Seuss's wife, Audrey used the foundation's money to help establish the Geisel Pavilion at Scripps Green Hospital in La Jolla, California where they lived, as well as the Geisel Chair in Biomedical Science at the Salk Institute.

Through the Dr. Seuss Foundation, Dr. Seuss's giving spirit continues to make a difference to this day.

CHAPTER 5
FUN FACTS

1. The Dr. Seuss Foundation was created by Dr. Seuss and his wife Audrey in 1958.

2. The foundation has given over $300 million to organizations, including schools and hospitals.

3. The foundation gave generously to Dartmouth College, where TDR. Seuss went to school.

4. Dr. Seuss loved animals and the environment, so the foundation supported the

Scripps Institution of Oceanography and the San Diego Zoo.

CHAPTER 6
A PERSONAL LIFE

Dr. Seuss was married twice in his lifetime. His first marriage was to Helen Palmer. They were married in 1927.

Helen was a classmate of his in Oxford, England. She was a writer and editor, and she supported her husband's career from the beginning. Helen noticed that Dr. Seuss was **exceptional** at drawing and once suggested that he focus on being an artist instead of becoming an English professor like he intended at the time. Her influence likely played a big role in why he ended up doing exactly that! She once said, "Ted's notebooks were always filled with these fabulous animals. So, I set to work diverting him; here was a man who could draw such pictures; he should be earning a living doing that."

Together, Helen and Dr. Seuss didn't have any children. Helen had

---

exceptional /ɪk-ˈsep-shə-nəl/ adjective: unusually good or exceptional <example: He is an exceptional student who excels in all his subjects.>

a medical condition and could not have children. They enjoyed their freedom and financial **security**. They often traveled together to inspiring locations that helped with Dr. Seuss's creative work.

Although not much is known about their personal relationship, it's clear that Helen was an important figure in Dr. Seuss's life and a strong support system for him. They remained together until Helen's death in 1967.

Audrey Stone Dimond met Dr. Seuss in La Jolla while he was still married to his first wife and she

---

security /sə-ˈkyü-r-ə-tē/ noun: the state of being protected or safe from harm or danger <example: The company's top priority is ensuring the security of its customers' data.>

was married to her first husband. She was trained as a nurse. She eventually divorced her first husband and fell in love with Dr. Seuss. The two married less than a year after Dr. Seuss's first wife died.

Audrey was also a supportive and creative partner for Dr. Seuss. The two of them had a happy and long marriage. They lived in a beautiful home in La Jolla, California, where Dr. Seuss continued to write and illustrate his beloved books. They also did not have children. They focused instead on Dr. Seuss's career and charitable giving.

Dr. Seuss and Audrey were married until Dr. Seuss's death in 1991. Following his death, she continued to work with the Dr. Seuss Foundation helping important causes and continuing his **legacy**.

---

legacy /ˈle-gə-sē/ noun: something that is handed down from an ancestor or predecessor <example: The company's legacy is a commitment to quality and customer satisfaction.>

CHAPTER 6
FUN FACTS

1. Dr. Seuss was married twice.

2. Dr. Seuss's first wife, Helen Palmer, was his college sweetheart that he met while attending Dartmouth College. She was an artist too.

3. Dr. Seuss and Helen Palmer experienced a personal tragedy when Helen's pregnancy ended in miscarriage. This experience deeply affected them, and they never had biological children.

4. Helen Palmer had two daughters from her previous marriage. Dr. Seuss was a stepfather to these two girls.

5. Dr. Seuss loved to travel as an adult and also lived in La Jolla, California, which is near San Diego.

CHAPTER 7
A LASTING LEGACY

Dr. Seuss has left an important and lasting legacy that spans generations. Through his imaginative and thought-provoking stories, he not only entertained readers but also taught important life lessons.

His books are celebrated for their ability to captivate the imaginations of people of all ages. With his playful language, clever rhymes, and creative illustrations, Dr. Seuss created a unique storytelling style that continues to be loved. His books encourage creativity and curiosity.

Beyond their entertainment value, Dr. Seuss's stories often contain deeper messages. Works like "The Lorax" address environmental issues, teaching the importance of caring for our planet. "The Sneetches" tackles themes of tolerance and acceptance, promoting empathy and understanding.

Dr. Seuss's lasting legacy is one of creativity. His stories continue to inspire curiosity and encourage a love for reading.

INSPIRATIONAL QUOTES

Quotes are like magical words that can lift your spirits and make you feel like you can conquer the world! They are short and powerful sentences that carry big messages. Quotes come from inspiring people who have experienced many things in life. They teach us valuable lessons, remind us to be brave, and encourage us to follow our dreams. So, whenever you need some inspiration or a little boost of confidence, just read a quote, and you'll feel like you can achieve anything! Here are a few quotes from Dr. Seuss to inspire you on your way!

" The more that you read, the more things you will know. The more that you learn, the more places you'll go."

" Don't cry because it's over, smile because it happened."

" You have brains in your head. You have feet in your shoes. You can steer yourself in any direction you choose."

" You know you're in love when you can't fall asleep because reality is finally better than your dreams."

" You have brains in your head. You have feet in your shoes. You can steer yourself any direction you choose."

" Today you are you, that is truer than true. There is no one alive who is youer than you."

" Why fit in when you were born to stand out?"

" Sometimes the questions are complicated, and the answers are simple."

" Don't cry because it's over, smile because it happened."

" Unless someone like you cares a whole awful lot, nothing is going to get better. It's not."

" You're off to Great Places! Today is your day! Your mountain is waiting, So... get on your way!"

" Be who you are and say what you feel, because those who mind don't matter and those who matter don't mind."

" To the world, you may be one person, but to one person you may be the world."

" Think and wonder, wonder and think."

" Sometimes you will never know the value of a moment until it becomes a memory."

" Oh, the things you can find if you don't stay behind!"

" A person's a person, no matter how small."

" You'll miss the best things if you keep your eyes shut."

" Simple it's not, I'm afraid you will find, for a mind-maker-upper to make up his mind."

" With your head full of brains and your shoes full of feet, you're too smart to go down any not-so-good street."

" And will you succeed? Yes, you will indeed! (98 and 3/4 percent guaranteed.)"

" From there to here, and here to there, funny things are everywhere."

" I like nonsense, it wakes up the brain cells. Fantasy is a necessary ingredient in living."

" You're in pretty good shape for the shape you are in."

BOOK
DISCUSSION

How do you think that Dr. Seuss's upbringing contributed to his success?

_____
_____
_____
_____
_____
_____
_____
_____
_____

What challenges did Dr. Seuss' face in his career, and how did he overcome them?

_____
_____

_____
_____
_____
_____
_____
_____
_____
_____

Why do you think Dr. Seuss's books are still popular today, many years after they were first published? What do you think makes them timeless, and how do they continue to resonate with kids of all ages?

_____
_____
_____
_____
_____
_____
_____
_____
_____

How did Dr. Seuss's hobbies contribute to his success?

_____
_____
_____
_____
_____
_____
_____
_____
_____
_____

GLOSSARY

charitable /ˈchar-ə-tə-bəl/ adjective: relating to giving money, help, or time to those in need <example: She is known for her charitable work in the community.>

decade /ˈdɛ-kād/ noun: a period of ten years <example: The last decade has seen significant changes in technology.>

establish /ɪ-ˈstab-lɪʃ/ verb: to create or set up a system, organization, or institution <example: They established a new company to produce the product.>

exceptional /ɪk-ˈsep-shə-nəl/ adjective: unusually good or exceptional <example: He is an exceptional student who excels in all his subjects.>

extracurricular /ˌek-strə-kə-'ri-kyə-lər/ adjective: outside the normal curriculum or routine <example: She participates in several extracurricular activities, including sports and music.>

forbidden /fər-'bɪ-dən/ adjective: not allowed by law, rule, or custom <example: Smoking is forbidden in this building.>

humor /'hyü-mər/ noun: the quality of being amusing or comical <example: He has a great sense of humor and always makes people laugh.>

illustrator /ɪ-ˈlʌs-trə-tər/ noun: a person who creates illustrations, especially for books or magazines <example: The book was illustrated by a famous illustrator.>

incorporate /ɪn-ˈkɔr-pə-rāt/ verb: to combine or join different elements or parts to form a single entity <example: The company incorporated new technology into its products.>

influential /ɪn-ˈflü-ən(t)-shəl/ adjective: having the power to influence or affect change <example: He is an influential person in the community, known for his leadership and ideas.>

legacy /'le-gə-sē/ noun: something that is handed down from an ancestor or predecessor <example: The company's legacy is a commitment to quality and customer satisfaction.>

marksman /'märk-mən/ noun: a person who is skilled in shooting, especially with a rifle <example: He is a marksman who competes in shooting competitions.>

prestigious /pre-'sti-jə-wəs/ adjective: respected and admired because of achievement, reputation, or social status <example: The university is one of the most prestigious in the country.>

professional /prə-'fə-shə-nəl/ adjective: relating to or belonging to a profession <example: She is a professional dancer who performs in ballets.>

pseudonym /'soō-də-nəm/ noun: a name used by a writer or artist instead of their real name <example: He writes under a pseudonym to protect his privacy.>

pursuits /pər-'sü-ts/ noun: an activity or interest that one enjoys and follows <example: Her hobbies include outdoor pursuits such as hiking and camping.>

security /sə-'kyü-r-ə-tē/ noun: the state of being protected or safe from harm or danger <example:

The company's top priority is ensuring the security of its customers' data.>

stable /ˈstā-bəl/ adjective: not likely to change or collapse; steady <example: The economy has been stable for several years.>

wit /wɪt/ noun: the ability to use words and ideas in a clever and amusing way <example: He is known for his quick wit and humor.>

SELECTED REFERENCES

Bernstein, Peter W. (1992). "Unforgettable Dr. Seuss". Reader's Digest Australia. Unforgettable. p. 192.

Cohen, Charles (2004). The Seuss, the Whole Seuss and Nothing but the Seuss: A Visual Biography of Theodor Seuss Geisel. Random House Books for Young Readers.

Fensch, Thomas (2001). The Man Who Was Dr. Seuss. Woodlands: New Century Books.

Geisel, Audrey (1995). The Secret Art of Dr. Seuss. Random House.

Jones, Brian Jay (2019). "Becoming Dr. Seuss: Theodor Geisel and the Making of an American Imagination." Dutton.

MacDonald, Ruth K. (1988). Dr. Seuss. Twayne Publishers.

Morgan, Judith; Morgan, Neil (1995). Dr. Seuss & Mr. Geisel. Random House.

Nel, Philip (2007). The Annotated Cat: Under the Hats of Seuss and His Cats. Random House.

Nel, Philip (2004). Dr. Seuss: American Icon. Continuum Publishing.

Pace, Eric (September 26, 1991). "Dr. Seuss, Modern Mother Goose, Dies at 87". The New York Times. New York City. Retrieved January 4, 2022.

Pease, Donald E. (2010). Theodor Seuss Geisel. Oxford University Press.

Scholl, Travis (March 2, 2012). "Happy birthday, Dr. Seuss!". St. Louis Post-Dispatch. St. Louis. Retrieved January 3, 2022.

Weidt, Maryann; Maguire, Kerry (1994). Oh, the Places He Went. Carolrhoda Books.

LETTER FROM THE AUTHOR

Dear Readers,

I hope you enjoyed this book and learned some take away that may help you as you continue to grow and make choices in life. Reading biographies of famous people can help us learn about ourselves and what decisions help and hurt people as they follow their dreams. If you enjoyed learning about this icon, you can read about more in our kids biographies series!

Happy learning and may your dreams come true!

All the best,

Adam Kent

COLLECT THE WHOLE
GET SMART BOOK SERIES

Here are just a few:

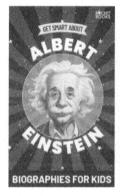  

ROCKET
BOOKS

Join our book club for free book offers. For more info email:

info@rocketkidsbookclub.com

Made in the USA
Las Vegas, NV
06 December 2023